MOHAMED SALAH

CLAIRE SIPI

FOOTBALL LEGENDS

MOHAMED SALAH

SCHOLASTIC

Published in the UK by Scholastic, 2026
Scholastic, Bosworth Avenue, Warwick, CV34 6UQ
Scholastic Ireland, 89E Lagan Road, Dublin Industrial Estate, Glasnevin, Dublin, D11 HP5F

ISBN 978 0702 34581 4

A CIP catalogue record for this book is available from the British Library.

Printed in the UK
Paper made from wood grown in sustainable forests and other controlled sources.

FSC www.fsc.org MIX Paper | Supporting responsible forestry FSC® C018072

10 9 8 7 6 5 4 3 2 1

www.scholastic.co.uk

For safety or quality concerns:
UK: www.scholastic.co.uk/productinformation
EU: www.scholastic.ie/productinformation

Contents

27 APRIL 2025

"Walk on, walk on
With hope in your heart
And you'll never walk alone
You'll never walk alone."

The sound was electrifying as the jubilant Liverpool fans cheered and sang, the stirring words of their club's anthem ringing across the Kop.

Mo Salah grinned at his teammates as they stood in a line on the pitch at Anfield, singing along with their fans. What a perfect end to a fantastic game. Liverpool had clinched their second Premier

League title with a fifteen-point lead and several games in hand. What a match! They had thrashed Tottenham Hotspur 5-1, guaranteeing them the prized silverware. With only a few more games to play to bring the season to an end, it wouldn't be long before they could hold up the trophy and celebrate their victory in style.

Luis Díaz, Alexis Mac Allister and Cody Gakpo delivered the first three goals in the first half, giving Liverpool the lead after an early goal from Spurs. Mo then scored their fourth goal in the second half, with Spurs player Destiny Udogie delivering an own goal to give the Reds their fifth goal and their dream win.

This was what it was all about. Mo's hard work, his courage, his dedication and passion and the support of his family had brought him here to this joyous moment. His journey to success had not been an easy one. Anfield's lush green football pitch was a far cry from the dusty, dry patch of ground in a small village in Egypt where Mo's childhood dreams of becoming a superstar footballer had begun...

SMALL VILLAGE, BIG DREAMS

On 15 June 1992, a boy named Mohamed Salah Hamed Mahrous Ghaly was born in a small farming village called Nagrig, in Egypt. Growing up, Mo lived in a modest home with his mum and dad, his three sisters, Mahy, Miram and Mona and his younger brother, Nasr. Like many Egyptian people, Mo and his family observed the customs and traditions of Islam, their religion. Mo was a happy and good-natured boy. He loved his family and his village and was often seen out and about feeding Nagrig's stray dogs. Mo had a kind soul and a big heart.

From the very beginning, football was a big

part of Mo's life. Both his father and uncle had played for a local amateur Nagrig team during their childhood, taking part in Egyptian youth competitions. A passion for football ran through Mo's family.

When Mo wasn't at school, feeding stray dogs or watching Champions League matches with his friends in the local café in Nagrig, he was out on the dusty streets of his village playing the beautiful game with his brother and his friends.

"Mama, can I go out and play football?" asked Mo.

"If you have finished your schoolwork," said his mother. "And take Nasr with you."

Nagrig's main street ran through fields growing wheat, alfalfa and watermelons, before reaching the centre of the village. Everything the small community needed was here – a school, a few shops, a café and the mosque – and, most importantly for Mo and Nasr, a dusty, dry patch of ground that was their football pitch, tucked between neglected blocks of flats and the village community hall. The rusty goalposts didn't have a net, but this didn't stop the boys playing out their dreams.

"One day I am going to be a superstar football player and travel the world," Mo told his brother.

Nasr watched his brother in awe as Mo ran down the pitch and placed a perfect goal between the rusty posts. Without doubt, Mo was one of the best players in their little group. He was super-fast and when he had the ball no one could catch him. With clever passes, crosses and quick turns Mo would score goal after goal.

When Mo watched a football match on the TV in the village café, he would study the tactics and tricks of his favourite players and then put these into practice when he played. His heroes were Zinedine Zidane from Real Madrid and Francesco Totti from Roma.

"I'm going to practise until I can dribble like Ryan Giggs, pass like Zinedine and shoot like Francesco," Mo told his friends.

"You're going to be a legend one day," his friends replied, impressed with Mo's skills.

When Mo watched or played football, he dreamed big and everything else faded away. He would travel the world and become an international professional football star, playing the sport he loved most to cheering crowds of fans, in some of the best stadiums that he had only seen on TV. Egypt would be proud of him.

But as soon as the game was over, Mo would come back down to earth with a bump and his dream seemed ridiculous. How was a seven-year-old boy from a small farming village ever going to become a world-class football star?

PRACTICE AND PASSION

Over the next few years, Mo continued to live and breathe football in his every waking moment. He spent hours watching the games in the top European leagues and competitions, and hours outside playing and practising new skills and tricks in school matches and community games.

Locally, people were starting to notice Mo's talent and his passion for the game. He was by far the best player among his peers and much better than some of the older boys he played with.

When World-Cup fever came to Nagrig in 2002, Mo was glued to all the games although

… hadn't qualified. Senegal's shocking win …ainst the reigning world champions, France, in the first match was an inspirational moment for ten-year-old Mo. If an African nation like Senegal could play like this, then why not Egypt?

"That could be me in years to come," he sighed to himself. "Leading Egypt to victory!"

Mo was particularly impressed by three of Brazil's top players. Ronaldo Luís Nazário de Lima, Rivaldo Vítor Borba Ferreira and Ronaldo de Assis Moreira (more commonly known as Ronaldo, Rivaldo and Ronaldinho) helped secure Brazil's place as winners of the 2002 World Cup. The 'Three Rs', the famous attacking football trio, became Mo's new football idols. They were everything that he wanted to be and, crucially, between them they scored lots of goals! Imitating their moves, Mo practised hard and was determined to do whatever it took to follow in the footsteps of his heroes.

The local youth football coach, Ghamry Abdel Hamid El Saadany, saw the passion and determination in Mo when he played.

"That boy has got what it takes!" he would tell

Mo's dad, as Mo tore through the opposition's defence in local league games and scored winning goals.

In practice sessions Ghamry helped Mo develop his skills, focusing on Mo's strengths – speed, dribbling and scoring goals. Mo could run fast and was brilliant at weaving past defenders with the ball. His shots were powerful, and he was great at putting the ball in the net.

"If Mo put as much effort into his schoolwork as his football, he would be top of his class!" joked Mo's dad. But he recognized the fire and passion in his son – football was in Mo's blood, and he saw it as his duty to do everything in his power to help Mo realize his dream.

If there was a football match to play, then Mo was there, sprinting down the field, dribbling the ball past the defenders, twisting and turning and then finishing with a powerful kick. He would shoot the ball past the surprised goalkeeper, who had inevitably dived the wrong way.

From the sidelines, year after year, Mo's dad watched his son play, filled with pride and shouting words of encouragement. As always, Mo was dominating the match.

"Son, these local games are not challenging enough for you," he told twelve-year-old Mo one day after his son had once again floored the opposition. "Your talent is going to waste here. I want to find you somewhere better to play and learn."

Mo was excited and very grateful that his family backed his dream of making it big in the world of football. With his dad, Mo travelled to Basyoun, about half an hour away from Nagrig, for a trial at Ittihad Basyoun football club.

"You've got this," said Mo's dad. Mo was nervous. Here he was, an unknown player who would be playing with better players than himself. But, as the ball was passed to him, he knew he could do it. He sped off down the pitch, weaving his way towards the goal. Kicking with his strong left foot, Mo powered the ball into the net past the stunned goalkeeper.

His new teammates gathered around him. "That was a great goal!"

Mo grinned as the coach came up to him. "Impressive, welcome to the team!"

THERE'S A SCOUT ABOUT

Mo was enjoying the challenges of playing in a bigger, more established team. If he worked hard this could be a stepping stone on to the next stage of his football journey and dream.

One day, when Mo was playing in a friendly match in his home village, a football scout from Cairo called Reda El-Mallah, who worked for Al Mokawloon football club, came to Nagrig to check out a young player called Sherif. El-Mallah travelled the country looking for young football talent for his Cairo-based club. As he stood on the sidelines watching the tall, athletic Sherif, another smaller player caught his attention.

AL MOKAWLOON FC

Nickname: Arab Contractors or the Contractors, Mountain Wolves, Meqawleen

Founded: 1973, by Osman Ahmed Osman, Egyptian contractor, engineer, entrepreneur and politician, as the official sporting club for his construction company, the Arab Contractors.

Stadium: Osman Ahmed Osman Stadium, also known as the Arab Contractors Stadium

Current league: Egyptian Premier League

Crest: a shield divided into 4 sections, with the full name of the football club written in Arabic in a white banner at the top of the shield. The top left section of the shield has a white silhouette of a football player running with a ball, on a yellow background with black vertical stripes. The top right section of the shield has a white silhouette of a rower on a blue background. The bottom left section of the shield has a white silhouette of a swimmer on a blue background. The bottom right section of the shield has a white silhouette of a basketball player with a ball, on a yellow background with black vertical stripes.

It was Mo! All the boys had been talking about the scout coming, and Mo, never one to miss an opportunity, had decided to play in the game to showcase his talents and try and impress the scout.

Despite his natural gift for football, Mo had never been a show-off. He was always humble and considerate of others; a great team player. However, on this day he knew that he had to shine. He remembered the words of his father and his coaches: "With hard work, practice and determination you have got what it takes to make it big."

So, when the ball was passed to him, touching it with his left foot, Mo powered it past the goalkeeper. GOAL! It was a great shot, but Mo didn't make a fuss about it. Instead, he quietly carried on playing, enjoying the game.

By the end of the match, Mo had scored a hat-trick. After the first goal, El-Mallah had turned his focus from Sherif on to Mo. He was impressed with Mo's playing, his speed and ball-handling skills, his impressive goal finishes and, most of all, his team spirit.

"Who is that player?" El-Mallah asked, pointing to Mo when the coach came over at the end of the match.

"You mean Sherif?" said the coach.

"No, sorry, I'm not interested in Sherif. I mean the boy who scored three goals," replied El-Mallah. "Now *he* has talent!"

Within a few weeks of El-Mallah's visit to Nagrig, Mo signed up with a youth club in Tanta, a city about a ninety-minute drive away. Mo couldn't believe his luck! Othmason Tanta youth football club was a bigger club than Ittihad Basyoun and they played at a higher level. Mo was so happy, and his family were very proud of him.

This was Mo's chance to really impress! And who knew? Maybe his big dream wasn't impossible after all.

4

AL MOKAWLOON

It was hard work fitting in school and travelling to Tanta for football matches and practice, but Mo took it in his stride. He loved playing for the club and over the next few years he put in the time improving his football skills.

Mo was now on the radar of the football scouts. Anyone watching the young boy play could see his passion and dedication. He was a talent waiting to be spotted.

Then, aged fourteen, Mo got an opportunity that was to change his life. He joined the youth team at Al Mokawloon, a team in the Egyptian Premier League.

Al Mokawloon football club was based in Cairo, 130 kilometres from Mo's home in Nagrig. This meant over a four-hour journey by bus each way! How was Mo going to manage this? He was too young to move away from home and live by himself.

After much discussion with the coaches, his school and his family, it was decided that Mo would make this eight-to-nine hour round journey. The only trouble was that Al Mokawloon trained five times a week, so Mo would have to make the journey there and back five times each week, even on school days! And there wasn't one direct bus to Cairo. He would have to change three or more times each way.

"How can I do this?" complained Mo to his mum and dad. "I'm going to miss so much school and I'm going to be exhausted all the time!"

But he knew that if he wanted to be a professional football player then he would have to make this huge sacrifice. It was a lot for a fourteen-year-old to take on. The buses were small and crowded, and some of the roads they travelled on were in disrepair and dangerous. It would be a long and gruelling journey and Mo was not looking forward to it, especially as he would have to get up very early every day.

To get to his 2.30 pm training session in Cairo, Mo had to catch a bus at 9.30 am each morning. In agreement with his school, Mo got special permission to start school at 7 am and leave at 9 am. Then he would dash for his first bus and start the long trek to Cairo.

Each training session was two to two-and-a-half hours long. Mo arrived already tired and stressed out. He then had to find the energy to focus completely on football, before dashing off again at the end of the session to start his journey home.

Exhausted and hungry, Mo would arrive home at about 10 pm at night, have a quick dinner and do his homework, and then drop into bed around midnight.

And at 6 am the next morning he would have to wake up and do it all again.

5

FOOTBALL LEGENDS

COMPETITION FOR POSITIONS

"It's amazing that you get to train and play with such a big team, Mo," said his friends. They were a little envious of him – until they heard about his gruelling schedule.

"It's exhausting, and the bus journey can be a bit scary sometimes," said Mo, "but if I want to become a superstar footballer like my heroes, then I know this will all be worth it in the end."

"*Habibi*, we are so proud of you," said Mo's mum and dad.

Mo was tired all the time, but no matter how difficult things were, he knew that he could not pass up this golden opportunity. Al Mokawloon was a great club for young players to develop their skills. And if he did well and progressed, he could move into the senior squad.

At first Mo was asked to play as a left-back defender. He wasn't happy with this position as it didn't allow him to utilize his speed, attack and goal-scoring skills. Mo loved scoring goals, and he knew he was good at putting the ball in the net.

But here at Al Mokawloon he wasn't the only talented player. There was a lot of competition for the right-wing attack positions, and Mo knew he would have to prove himself and show the coaches just what he could do if he wanted a chance at playing in his preferred position.

Mo wasn't one to complain. He kept his head down and worked hard, practising all the hours he could, but after a while he couldn't hide his disappointment any more. He desperately wanted to be scoring goals.

One day, at the end of another hard training session, his coach, Hamdi Nooh, found Mo in tears.

"What's wrong, Mo?" Hamdi enquired.

"I'm struggling to play in defence," sighed Mo. "I've

always played in an attack position, and now I can't score goals like I used to."

Hamdi liked Mo. He could see the budding talent in the boy. "OK, next game I will put you on the right wing so you can show me what you can do."

As Hamdi watched Mo sprint and weave down the pitch, he saw how comfortable and natural Mo was as a right-winger, and how great he was at scoring goals.

He told Mo he was going to move him to this new position.

"Thank you," cried Mo, grinning widely. "You won't regret this!"

The long days and tiring journeys didn't seem so bad now that Mo was playing where he was meant to be.

Hamdi continued to push Mo hard in their training sessions. He didn't want this young talent to become complacent.

"If you want to become a champion you've always got to be improving your skills and game strategies," he told Mo.

Mo knew this was true. If he wanted to stand out then he needed to keep upping his game. He had to shine! Mo was determined more than ever to show the coaches at Al Mokawloon just how bright a star he was going to be.

"This is my chance. I know I can do this," he promised himself on yet another long bus journey home.

6

FOOTBALL LEGENDS

SENIOR SQUAD SKILLS

"I want you to start training with the senior squad," Hamdi Nooh told Mo one afternoon.

This was music to Mo's ears. He was ready to take the next step. Following Hamdi's advice, Mo had worked hard on improving his ball skills using his right foot which wasn't as strong as his left one. This had given him an edge, because he could now switch feet and trick the defence.

The manager of the senior squad, Mohamed Radwan, had been watching Mo closely and he was impressed with the young player's skills and attitude to learning.

"I think Mo has huge potential, and I would like to give him a chance to play a match with the senior squad," he said.

When Mo was called on as a sub for Al Mokawloon's first team's last three games of the season he jumped for joy. Playing his best football, he impressed the team and the fans.

"I'm going to show them that I am ready for this," Mo told himself.

On 3 May 2010, just over a month before his eighteenth birthday, Mo was promoted to Al Mokawloon's first team. After four years of hard training with the youth squad, and the hours and hours of gruelling bus journeys, all his sacrifices had paid off.

Mo was given a contract and a room near Al Mokawloon's Osman Ahmed Osman Stadium. No more bus journeys and, most importantly, a big step closer to his dream!

THE OSMAN AHMED OSMAN STADIUM

Also known as the Arab Contractors Stadium or Al Mokawloon Al Arab Stadium, this stadium, located in Nasr City, Cairo, is the home stadium of Egyptian football club Al Mokawloon Al Arab. It has a seating capacity of 35,000 and is mostly used for football matches. It opened in 1979 and has a grass surface.

7

BEST FRIENDS

"Come on, Mo," laughed Mohamed Elneny. "Get your boots on and let's get to practice and show them what we can do!"

Al Mokawloon had signed another young player to the first team. Mohamed Elneny (another Mo) was the same age as Mo, and the two young lads soon became great friends.

Although Mo loved living close to the club training ground, and he certainly didn't miss the long bus journeys, it was hard being away from his family. So having the friendship of Mohamed was just what he needed.

Mohamed and Mo shared the same dream of becoming international football stars and were determined to stand out in their first season at Al Mokawloon. All summer they practised hard, working on their skills and preparing for the start of the Egyptian Premier League season.

EGYPTIAN PREMIER LEAGUE

The Egyptian Premier League was founded in 1948. It is the top tier football league in Egypt, run by the Egyptian Football Association. Made up of 18 teams, it operates on a promotion and relegation system with Egypt's Second Division A. The 2025/2026 season has seen the temporary introduction of 21 teams, using a two-phase system. In phase one, the teams play each other once, after which they are split into two groups. In phase two, the teams who finished in first to seventh place play for the championship, and the remaining 14 teams play to avoid relegation. The League is sponsored by Nile Developments and so is sometimes called the Nile League.

Mohamed Radwan had taken Mo under his wing. He was impressed with Mo's discipline, energy, drive and humbleness. This was rare in a younger player with such talent. He wanted to harness this potential and help make Mo the star he knew he could be.

Training was strenuous but Mo knew that he couldn't afford to get lazy or complacent. He was aware that he had the skills and talent, but he also knew that he had to keep improving if he wanted to make it into the big leagues.

"The coach wants me to try to dribble the ball less and run more, so I can get behind defence to score more goals," Mo told his best friend Mohamed.

"That sounds like a great plan, Mo," replied Mohamed. "You're so fast you can definitely outrun the defence!"

As the first season progressed, Mo and Mohamed got to play regularly. Their coaches wanted to put their skills to use – Mo in attack and Mohamed in midfield. However, the team wasn't winning any of their matches.

This didn't stop Mo and Mohamed. They were more determined than ever to show their fans, their teammates and the other teams in the league that they wouldn't go down without a fight.

Mo's first goal for the league came on 25 December 2010 when Al Mokawloon played the champion team of the league, Al Ahly. Remembering the coach's advice, Mo got behind the defence, sprinted away and finished with a superb shot, powering the ball into the back of the net straight past the stunned goalkeeper.

The fans went wild! Mo was ecstatic. He waved his arms in the air and then knelt on the pitch and kissed the grass. What a moment! This was what it was all about.

Although Al Mokawloon stayed at the bottom of the Egyptian Premier League that season, Mo and his new friend Mohamed continued to play hard and score goals, showing their team and their fans that they meant business.

They were stars in the making!

8

FOOTBALL LEGENDS

INTERNATIONAL EXPERIENCE

"I can't believe we are going to Colombia!" cried Mo excitedly.

It was the summer of 2011, and Radwan had just told Mo and Mohamed Elneny that they had been chosen to represent Egypt in the Under-20 World Cup. This was a big deal for the two young players. They would be making their senior debut at an international level.

"It's going to be so cool," sighed Mohamed. "We're going to be playing top teams like Brazil and Argentina!"

Mo knew a lot was riding on his performance.

It was at tournaments like this that football scouts from all over the world would be looking for talent for the big clubs. It was still his dream to play in the English Premier League one day.

Egypt's first game was against Brazil. It was a tough game, but Egypt managed to equalize to make the final score 1-1. Egypt's football coach, Diaa El-Sayed, was proud of his team.

"You did well," he told the lads. "Keep up this energy!"

But Mo wasn't happy. He'd missed an opportunity to score a goal.

"I can't seem to find my pace," Mo told Diaa. "I should be scoring goals."

"I think you are trying too hard," replied Diaa. "Your form is good and you don't have to be scoring all the goals for the team. You are a playmaker too."

Mo loved scoring goals more than anything, but it was true, he wasn't the only one on the team, and he was excellent at creating opportunities for his teammates to score goals.

"Don't be too much in your own head," Diaa advised. "You are a natural. Stop thinking about only scoring goals and you will see, it will happen."

Mo tried to take the coach's advice, but he just couldn't find the net in their next few games. The team, however, made it into the round of sixteen. They were up against Argentina. This was a make-or-break match.

Mo wasn't hopeful. "We're not going to make it through," he told Mohamed.

"Come on, Mo, don't give up on us," said Mohamed. "Remember your dream! Remember what the coach said."

Egypt were two goals down when they were awarded a penalty. Mo quickly stepped up to take it. He had to do this. Blocking out everything else around him, Mo focused on the ball at his feet. With a quick flick of his foot and cool determination, he fired the ball straight past the goalkeeper. What a goal!

Fired up, Mo was back on form. He played his best for the rest of the game, but in the end Argentina won the game 2-1 and Egypt were out of the competition.

Mo was disappointed with himself, but he knew he couldn't waste time wallowing in self-pity. There would be other opportunities, and maybe, just maybe, one day he would help make his national team world champions!

DISAPPOINTMENT AND DETERMINATION

Back in Cairo again, it wasn't long before Mo got another chance to get himself noticed in the wider football world.

Mo and Mohamed Elneny from Egypt's Under-23s were picked for the team to play in the African Cup of Nations qualifiers against Sierra Leone and Niger.

"We've got this!" shouted Mohamed happily.

"Yeah! Watch out world, here we come!" cried Mo.

After a disappointing loss to Sierra Leone, Egypt weren't going to make it through to the 2012 finals.

However, Mo and Mohamed were determined to do better in the match against Niger and show their country what they could do.

With their teammates they played brilliantly. With one goal in hand, Mo sped down the pitch and scored a brilliant second goal to bring the final score to 2-0 against Niger. This was Mo's first senior international goal.

"That was brilliant!" roared Mohamed.

Mo grinned at his friend. It was moments like this that made all the hard work worthwhile.

On the back of this win, Egypt went on to play in the African Under-23 Championship and secured a place in the semi-final where they would play against Morocco. Would this be their crowning moment?

Two goals down to Morocco only minutes into the game, Egypt didn't look like they could make it.

"Come on! Keep it together!" shouted Mo. "We can do this."

Fired up and wanting to impress, Mo sprinted down the field and, moments later, scored a fantastic goal. If Egypt could hold their nerve, they might have a chance. But then Morocco scored another goal, securing their place in the final against Gabon.

Although Mo and his teammates were disappointed, their 2-0 win against Senegal in the third-place playoff secured them a place in the 2012 Olympic Games that were going to be held in London.

FOOTBALL AT THE OLYMPICS

Men's football was first played at the 1900 Olympics held in Paris. Until the 1908 Olympics, only amateur club teams could compete. After this date, national teams could play. Professional players were allowed in 1984, but from 1992, players in the men's teams had to be under the age of 23, with an 'exception rule' that allowed three older players per team. This rule was introduced by FIFA, the world football governing body, so that the Olympic football tournament wouldn't compete with the men's World Cup tournament.

Women's football was only introduced in 1996, without age restrictions. Women's Olympic football is classed as a full international competition for senior players and is the second most important competition for women after their World Cup.

For both the men's and the women's Olympic matches, two halves of 45 minutes each are played. The tournament has a group stage and a knockout stage like the World Cup.

EYES ON EUROPE

People were talking about Mo Salah and his footballing talent was being recognized. The kid from the small village was now making a name for himself, nationally and internationally.

"You're like a goal-scoring machine!" laughed his coach. They were back in Cairo and Mo was scoring goal after goal for Al Mokawloon.

Other big Egyptian clubs like Al Ahly and Zamalek had been keeping a close eye on Mo's performance, and they were vying for the young star, offering him fame and money to sign up with them.

Mo was flattered that his talent was getting

recognition, but he was still dreaming of bigger things. He wanted to play in Europe and, hopefully, one day achieve his top ambition, which was to play in the UEFA Champions League like his childhood football heroes.

"Don't give up on your dreams or ambitions, Mo," Radwan advised him. "You've got the drive and the talent to make it big in Europe. You're too good to stay and play in the Egyptian Premier League. You are one of the most exciting players we have."

Mo and Mohamed Elneny often talked about playing for a big European club.

"If we make it, we will get to play in the Champions League," sighed Mohamed.

"I think we can do it," replied Mo. "I know I have got options here, but I don't want to settle for second best."

With support from his family, his best friend and his coach, and with the backing of the Al Mokawloon football club, Mo decided it was time to change things up.

Events soon forced him to take action. On 1 February 2012, seventy-four people were killed and many injured in violent clashes between rival football fans in the Egyptian city of Port Said, following an Egyptian Premier League football match between Al Masry and Al Ahly. As a result of this tragic riot, the Egyptian government shut down the domestic football league for two years. This decision pushed Mo into acting sooner rather than later.

"We're going to Basel, Switzerland," Radwan told Mo at the beginning of March.

The Egyptian Under-23 team had been invited to play in a friendly match against Basel. Mo was anxious but excited. Could this be the start of his European adventure?

As the match progressed, Mo played all his best moves and tricks, scoring two goals. Basel football club were impressed by his skills and his speed on the pitch.

"I want this boy," said Bernhard Heusler, the president of the club. "Let's sign him up before someone else does."

In July 2012, Basel signed Mo for 2.25 million pounds!

Mo couldn't believe it. "Am I really going to play in Europe?"

"That's amazing! You know that Basel regularly

play in the Champions League and Europa League," said Mohamed. "I'm so happy for you, but I'm going to miss you, my friend."

FC BASEL 1893

Nickname: FCB, RotBlau (RedBlue, their home colours)
Founded: 1893
Stadium: St Jakob-Park
Current leagues: Swiss Super League, Swiss Cup
Crest: a shield, outlined in gold and divided in half. The left half is red, and the right half is blue. The stylized, intertwined letters 'FCB', in gold, fill the centre of the shield. FCB stands for the club's name, 'Football Club Basel'. A gold football sits on the edge of the left side of the shield.

11

FOOTBALL LEGENDS

LONDON CALLING

Before Mo could settle into his new life in Basel, another adventure awaited him: the 2012 Olympic Games in London.

Mo had always wanted to visit London. He'd heard so much about the busy, cosmopolitan city and couldn't wait to see it for himself.

"You know what is going to be so cool?" said Mo as he, Mohamed and the rest of the team prepared for their journey to England, "We're going to get to play at some of the top English clubs' stadiums! And if we make it through to the final, we'll be playing in Wembley Stadium."

It had always been a dream of Mo's to play at Wembley.

Egypt was to play Belarus, New Zealand and Brazil in their group stage.

2012 Olympic Games, London

Group stage

Brazil 3-2 Egypt

Egypt 1-1 New Zealand

Egypt 3-1 Belarus

Quarter final

Japan 3-0 Egypt

Brazil, one of the favourites to win, was going to be the real challenge, and in the first half of the game they destroyed Egypt with a three-goal lead. Mo didn't come on until the second half. He didn't want to see his team defeated and he was ready for action.

His teammate Mohamed Aboutrika scored the first of Egypt's goals, and then it was Mo's turn.

Mohamed Elneny set up a perfect pass and then Mo, with his now famous goal-scoring abilities, kicked the ball into the net. The fans went wild! Unfortunately Egypt couldn't produce another goal and Brazil won the match.

Undeterred, Mo went on to score a goal in each of Egypt's next two group-stage games against New Zealand and Belarus, helping his team secure a place in the quarter-finals, much to the delight of their fans in the stadium and those back home watching the game on TV.

Although Egypt didn't win their match against Japan, and Mo didn't get to play at Wembley, he was proud of his performance and his three great goals. He could go back to Basel with his head held high.

And London had been everything he had dreamed of. Maybe, one day soon, he would be travelling back to England to play in one of the top Premier League teams and finally get to score a goal in the famous Wembley Stadium.

12

ALL CHANGE

The move to Basel was not easy.

Twenty-year-old Mo didn't know anyone. He had no friends, and he was living in a different country a long way from home where no one spoke his language, Arabic.

"I know this is what I wanted," Mo complained to his parents when he called them, "and I love that I am playing in Europe, but I feel so lonely."

"You will get used to it, my son," his dad replied gently. "We are so proud of you. This is your dream and you are making it come true, never forget that."

Mo had always known that the path to success would not be easy, but sometimes it was hard to remember that in those vulnerable moments. However, he was not one to give up that easily.

"Baba, Mama, I will do what it takes," he reassured his parents. "You will see me play in the Champions League one day!"

When he wasn't training, Mo explored the city, familiarizing himself with his new home. He enrolled in English classes and learnt some Swiss German so that he could understand his new manager.

Mo discovered that the style of playing football in Europe was very different to what he was used to back home. The game was much more physical and was played at a faster pace. But if there was one thing Mo was good at, it was learning and adapting to new things and situations.

With the encouragement of his new coach and teammates, Mo began to relax into his new life. He trained hard to improve his stamina for the matches and practised for hours to refine his technique and skills. He was going to make this work. He was going to keep pushing for the top and become the legend he knew he could be.

One day Mo's friend Mohamed Elneny called him.

"Mo, you are never going to believe this!" Mohamed cried. "I've been signed for Basel, and I'll be joining you soon."

A huge grin spread across Mo's face. "That's fantastic! It's going to be great having you here. You're going to love it, and I can show you around."

This was the best news ever. Living in Europe was going to be a lot easier and better with his best friend by his side.

13

FOOTBALL LEGENDS

SETTLING IN

Mo's first season at Basel was going well.

He'd adapted his techniques to playing with his new teammates, and he was beginning to feel like a valued member of the team now. He was keen to show them how good a goal scorer he was.

That chance came in an early game in the season against FC Lausanne. As Mo kicked the ball past the goalkeeper with his usual flair and speed, the fans screamed out his name in delight.

What an incredible feeling! *This must be what it is like to be a superstar,* Mo thought. As his teammates gathered around him and the fans chanted his name, Mo dropped to his knees and kissed the grass. He would always be grateful for the wonderful opportunities that had blessed his life, and he would never forget to be thankful for the support and love of his family, friends, and his team and fans – no matter how big a star he became. This was his way of showing everyone just how thankful he was.

Back in training, Murat Yakin, Basel's manager, was watching his new player closely. He could see the fire in Mo and how driven he was. If it had been down to Mo, he would have played for the full ninety minutes of every one of Basel's matches, but Murat had other ideas.

"I hate sitting on the bench," Mo moaned after another match where he had only been on the pitch for a short time. "It feels like a punishment."

"But you need to rest, and it's my job to make sure you don't burn out," replied Murat. "Trust me, I know how to get the best out of my players."

This was true. Basel were one of the best Swiss clubs and they were always winning trophies. Playing with them, Mo would get a lot of exposure to the top football clubs in Europe.

"You will get your chances to work your magic,

Mo," continued Murat. "Just give it time, be patient and keep working hard."

Basel won the Super League at the end of that season for the third time in a row. Although Mo hadn't scored as many goals as he would have liked to, he knew he had contributed to that win as part of the team.

Enjoying the celebrations in the city with his best friend Mohamed Elneny, Mo was more determined than ever to make his name in Europe. With Basel he was getting to play against some of the top teams in Europe, and this was how he was going to get noticed.

14

EUROPA LEAGUE

Mo's dream of playing in the Champions League in his first season at Basel was short-lived, as they were knocked out in the final qualifying round.

"Next season, Mo," said Mohamed Elneny. "I'm sure we will be playing in the Champions League then. Keep your spirits up."

"Yes, you're right," replied Mo. "Let's put all our energy into the Europa League. We're going to be playing some great teams."

Basel got through to the Europa League quarter-final. Mo and Mohamed couldn't wait to get on the pitch. They were going to be playing against

Tottenham Hotspur at White Hart Lane in England. This was a huge moment for them. After an exciting and well-fought match, Basel and Tottenham Hotspur were locked in a stalemate – 2-2. This meant Basel would get to play them again at home.

As the match progressed in Basel's home stadium, St Jakob-Park, Mo set his sights on showing everyone just what a star he was. Tottenham Hotspur had taken the lead, but then Mo got an opportunity to score. Sprinting as fast as he could, he got the ball and powered it into the net. This was his first Europa League goal! The fans were going wild.

Mo didn't get another chance at goal, but the match ended in a 4-4 draw. After no more goals for either side in the extra thirty minutes played, Basel won the match on penalties 4-1. Mo hadn't taken any of the penalties, but his team was through to the semi-finals, and he would be playing in a match against Chelsea at Stamford Bridge!

As the first half of the match against Chelsea was coming to an end, Mo's second chance at a goal in the Europa League came. He wasn't going to miss it. As the goalkeeper dived to save the goal, Mo fired the ball high, right over him, and into the back of the net.

"Come on!" roared Mo at his teammates. "This is our shot at the final."

Although Basel pulled out all the stops, Chelsea eventually won the match 3-1. Mo couldn't hide his disappointment. He'd been playing at the top of his game, and this time it hadn't been enough.

But all was not lost. Important people in the football world were talking about Mohamed Salah. His performance and impressive goal scoring had not gone unnoticed, and it wouldn't be long before events would change Mo's life for ever.

15

FOOTBALL LEGENDS

RISING STAR

The 2013/14 season was upon them and Basel qualified for the Champions League.

"I can't believe we're in the same group as Chelsea," Mo said, as he and Mohamed Elneny discussed tactics and game plans for their second chance at beating Chelsea, and this time in the Champions League.

"I'm excited to be playing in London again," Mohamed grinned. "And it'll be even better if we thrash them!"

As the Basel team walked down the tunnel at Stamford Bridge and on to the pitch to cheers from their fans, Mo turned to his teammates.

"This is our chance to prove we are better than them," he said. "Let's show the world just who we are."

Basel were ready for this match; they had been practising hard. And Mo was feeling confident. He'd been playing with Basel for over a year now and he knew that he was getting better all the time. He had put in the work and it was showing.

Chelsea scored the first goal, but then Mo spotted his chance. Calmly and with precision, he booted the ball into the net. It was the perfect goal. The fans went wild, and the Basel players lifted Mo into the air. Mo beamed as he soaked in the incredible atmosphere. This is where he was meant to be! But remembering how he had got there, he dropped to the ground and kissed the grass, never forgetting to be thankful.

Basel were on a roll, and with a second goal from Marco Streller, they finished the game 2-1.

As the team flew back home, they chatted excitedly about the return match at their stadium in a month's time. They were confident that they could beat Chelsea again.

And they did! What a game it was. With a few minutes left to play, neither team had managed to score a goal. And then came Mo's moment to shine. He took possession of the ball and, using the tricks he had practised many hours to perfect, weaved down the field towards the goal…

POW! The ball flew into the net as Chelsea's goalkeeper dived to the ground. GOAL!

The stadium reverberated with cheers and whistles. Basel had done it, and Mo's fantastic goal had cinched it for them.

"You were on fire today, Mo!" Bernhard Heusler, Basel's club president, said, shaking his star player's hand. "Keep this up. You're really making a name for yourself. There's a lot of chatter about you."

Several of the big English league clubs had been watching Mo for a while and were impressed by his superb performances. Liverpool Football Club was keen to sign Mo, but Basel had already turned down their offer. They knew they were in a good position to bargain for a more lucrative deal for their star player.

And that offer wasn't long in arriving.

16

BIG CHANGES

Mo was tired but contented. It had been a long year of highs and lows. Everyone at the club was pleased with how Mo had improved in just two seasons, and he knew that the hours of practice and playing were beginning to pay off. For every disappointment there had been a better high. Mo had honed his skills. He had listened to his coaches and put their advice into play. He had worked hard and never let his dream of stardom make him too big for his boots, on or off the field. As long as he was scoring goals he was happy.

And now other European clubs wanted him!

Mo couldn't wait to talk to his family about

everything. As most of Europe shut down for the holidays in December, Mo was heading back home to Egypt for a well-deserved break with his family and for a very exciting occasion.

Mo was getting married! Magi Sadeq was his childhood sweetheart. They had met at school and kept in touch ever since. In a small celebration on 17 December 2013, Mo and Magi tied the knot!

Mo loved being a star on the football pitch, but outside of this he was a very private person. He didn't want people to know everything about him, his family or friends. People could ask him anything about his football life and he was happy to share that with his fans and the rest of the world. But he wanted to keep his private life just that – private.

His wedding wasn't a star-studded event splashed all over the media. In a small, private ceremony in his village Mo married Magi. Mo the footballer was still just that, a footballer. And now, as a married man, he returned to Basel in January to continue being a footballer with the blessing and support of his family.

Big changes were ahead.

Chelsea's manager, José Mourinho, wanted to

sign Mo. He'd not been happy when Chelsea had lost to Basel twice, but nevertheless he had been very impressed with Mo's goal-scoring abilities. And Liverpool, under the management of Brendan Rodgers, were bidding again.

Mo was torn. It was his dream come true to be part of an English Premier League football team, and now several teams wanted him! He was very tempted by Liverpool's offer, they were a fantastic team after all, and Mo had been a fan of theirs as a child, watching their games on the TV in the little café in his home village.

But then Chelsea put in a better offer. They had more money to spend, and Basel football club were keen for Mo to accept. So, in January 2014, Mo signed with Chelsea for an estimated eleven million pounds.

"You've made it!" cried Mohamed Elneny. "You are going to be living the dream in England. What am I going to do without you? I'm going to miss you so much."

"I'm going to miss you, too," Mo said. "But I've got to do this. This is where my life has been leading."

FOOTBALL LEGENDS

17

HEADING TO ENGLAND

Everything was happening very quickly.

Mo had just started to get used to his life in Basel, and now he was moving to London to start playing with his new team, Chelsea. He was going to miss his Basel friends, especially Mohamed Elneny, but at least this time he could speak the language and, best of all, he would be with his wife, Magi.

The newlyweds were excited to be starting a new life in London, but they had underestimated how overwhelming life in a big capital city could be. Basel had been an eye-opener for Mo when he had arrived there, but London was something different again. Everywhere was so noisy and busy, a far cry from the quiet, dusty streets of Nagrig.

"We'll soon settle, Mo," said Magi. "Don't worry. We've got each other and I'm here to support you. This is your dream, and you've worked so hard to achieve all of this."

Mo knew Magi was right. It would work out, and he had already overcome harder obstacles on his football journey so far. This was his dream and he was going to live it to the full.

But as the 2013/14 season came to an end, and Mo spent a lot of time on the bench rather than playing in matches. He began to grow very anxious.

"This is not what I signed up for," he told Magi. "I need to be playing."

José Mourinho had told Mo that he wouldn't play him in every game, but Mo hadn't banked on playing as little as he had. He felt restless and was worried that he would lose his touch if he didn't play more.

He was also finding fitting into the team much harder than he had imagined. He was surrounded by confident, world-class players, who were used to all the media attention that came with being a megastar in a top league team. And English football was even more physical than playing for Basel. Everyone seemed so powerful and strong. Would he be able to use his speed to get through the defenders in the English teams?

When Mo tried to talk to José about his worries, José just said he had to give it time and keep working on perfecting his skills. His chance would come.

But Mo was impatient. How could he be the star he wanted to be if he wasn't playing? And by the time the 2014/15 season started, Mo had completely lost his confidence. He couldn't find his form in the few games he played in and he wasn't scoring goals.

"I don't know what's wrong with me!" Mo moaned to Mohamed Elneny when he called his friend. "I can't score goals, and I always score goals! That's what I'm about."

Mohamed sympathized with his friend. "You've got to hang in there," he advised. "I'm sure you'll get to play soon."

But Mo didn't, and he knew he wasn't making a good impression on his team. As the new season dragged on, Mo knew things would have to change. This was a setback in his dream, but he wasn't prepared to let his dream die.

18

FOOTBALL LEGENDS

FINDING HIS FEET

When the transfer window opened in January 2015, Mo decided to take matters into his own hands. He couldn't sit around any more hoping for a miracle. He needed – and wanted – to play more football.

Chelsea would often loan out their young players to other clubs in Europe for them to get more experience. Mo approached José Mourinho and asked if he could go out on loan. He wanted to show his manager that he still had his passion and drive and the will to improve his game.

José agreed. In February 2015, Mo was sent on loan to Italy to play for Fiorentina.

Mo felt his spirits lifting as he and Magi packed up to move to Florence with their little daughter, Makka.

"I think this is going to be good for me," Mo told his parents when he called home. "This is my chance to recharge and get a fresh start and find my goal-scoring feet again."

And Mo did!

Match after match he scored impressive goal after impressive goal. His confidence was back, and it showed as he sprinted about the pitch, getting past the defenders and into the right position to receive a pass, before finishing with his famous powerful kick to get the ball in the back of the net. His new team were impressed.

"I'm back!" he told Mohamed Elneny after he scored against Tottenham Hotspur in the Europa League and Inter Milan in Serie A.

As he continued to set Italian football on fire, Mo only hoped that José Mourinho was watching. He'd found his form and his star was shining again. Italian football had saved him.

Mo was enjoying football again after his slump at Chelsea, and when the season finished, Fiorentina didn't want to see him go. When Mo heard that José didn't want him back yet, he would have happily stayed at Fiorentina on loan, but another Italian club had been watching him closely and they wanted this goal-scoring machine for themselves!

19

ANOTHER MOVE

AS Roma football club negotiated a deal with Chelsea to have Mo on loan for a year for the 2015/16 season, and Mo and Magi packed once again to move to Rome.

Mo was excited. "If they like me, there's a chance they will sign me up permanently," he told Magi. "And I'm going to get to play with Francesco Totti!"

Francesco was one of Mo's all-time childhood heroes. He couldn't believe this turn of fortune. This was a dream come true. Mo remembered telling his school friends back in Nagrig that he was going to be a star and score goals just like Francesco. And now he was going to get to play alongside his hero in real life, and in the Champions League!

Life couldn't have been better. Mo continued to impress his team and club, scoring goals in crucial matches throughout the season.

Roma's manager, Luciano Spalletti, called Mo over. "We want to sign you up permanently. You are one of the most talented and driven players I have ever worked with."

And on 3 August 2016, AS Roma signed Mo for a whopping thirteen-and-a-half million pounds.

AS ROMA

Nickname: I Giallorossi (the Yellow and Reds), I Lupi (the Wolves), La Magica (the Magic One)
Founded: 1927
Stadium: Stadio Olimpico
Current League: Serie A
Crest: (updated in June 2025) a shield, divided in half horizontally and surrounded by a yellow border. The top half has an

image of the Lupa Capitolina – the wolf that nurtured Romulus and Remus in Rome's foundation myth – on a yellow background. The bottom half has the stylized, intertwined letters 'ASR', in gold, on a deep red background. ASR stands for the club's name, 'Associazione Sportiva Roma'.

Mo couldn't have been happier. He knew he still had a lot of work to do to improve his skills and game tactics, but he was in the best place to learn. As the new season kicked off, Mo continued to score goals, running circles round opposition defence. In a match against Bologna in the Serie A tournament in November that year, Mo not only scored all three goals to win the game, but it was his first-ever career hat-trick at club level.

Mo was AS Roma's second top goal scorer with fifteen goals in his first season with them. Everyone was so impressed with Mo's outstanding performance that he was voted Player of the Season.

Magi hugged her husband close. "I'm so proud

of you, Mo. Look at how far you have come."

Back in Nagrig, Mo's family were following his meteoric rise with pride.

"I always knew our boy had it in him!" sighed Mo's dad happily. "He's Egypt's star."

20

CLIMBING THE LADDER

The following year, 2017, started well. Mo was playing some of his best football with AS Roma, and Egypt qualified for the African Cup of Nations.

Mo loved playing for his country, especially as he would be playing alongside his best friend, Mohamed Elneny. Mohamed had now left Basel and was playing for Arsenal.

Mo was happy for his friend. "How's it going in England?" he asked Mohamed.

"Ah, it's great, I'm loving it," cried Mohamed. "I can't believe we're both living the dream!"

"Well, let's see if we can make our African dream come true and win this tournament," Mo laughed. "If we can do well here, then World Cup 2018 here we come!"

Mo, Mohamed and the rest of the Egyptian squad had been practising hard. After a rocky start in their first few games, they picked up the pace. Mo and Mohamed made a good pair. Mohamed knew when to pass to Mo, setting him up for scoring goals.

When Egypt made it to the final the fans went wild. Mo had scored another great goal in the semi-final against Burkina Faso.

EGYPT NATIONAL SQUAD

- Egypt is Africa's oldest national football team. It was first created in 1920 to compete in the Olympics held in Belgium.
- Egypt has won the Africa Cup of Nations a record seven times (1957, 1959, 1986, 1998, 2006, 2008, 2010).
- Egypt has made three appearances (1934,

1990 and 2018) in the FIFA World Cup, being the first-ever African and Middle Eastern team to qualify.

- The Egypt National Squad use the Borg El Arab Stadium in Alexandria and the Cairo International Stadium as their home stadiums.
- The Egypt National Squad are known by their nickname of the Pharaohs.

Now the Pharaohs would have to face Cameroon.

"We can do this, lads!" shouted Mo.

Mohamed scored a brilliant goal in the first half after an excellent pass from Mo, giving Egypt the lead 1-0. But then Cameroon equalized and, in the last few minutes of the game, they scored another goal to win the tournament.

Egypt had played well, but the team was disappointed.

"Learn from your mistakes and move on," their coach said.

Mo sighed. They could still qualify for the

2018 World Cup, and he knew he had to keep moving forward if he wanted to be a superstar. Superstars never gave up and he never would.

Back in Rome, Mo kept his promise to himself. He was learning new skills and game tactics all the time, pushing himself harder with each match and playing at the top of his game.

This didn't go unnoticed. Liverpool Football Club had wanted to sign Mo up for several years, having lost out to Chelsea back in 2014. Now their new manager, Jürgen Klopp, saw another opportunity to get this star player.

Mo loved playing for AS Roma, but he knew that he could not stay still if he wanted to win trophies and climb the ladder to football stardom. And AS Roma weren't winning trophies that season. Playing for Liverpool, one of the biggest and most famous clubs in the world, would be a huge step up and a fantastic opportunity.

So, when Liverpool bid almost thirty-seven million pounds for Mo, he knew he could not turn this once-in-a-lifetime offer down.

Mo was Liverpool's most expensive signing at the time. Jürgen really wanted this young player.

"I will give you every opportunity to play," Jürgen told Mo. "Your talent won't be wasted here, and you certainly won't be sitting on the bench."

"You won't be sorry, I promise you," Mo replied confidently.

Once again, Mo's life was about to change. Moving to England to play for Liverpool would be the making of Mo. This time he could really become the football icon of his dreams!

When Mo told his family they were over the moon for him.

"Son, we couldn't be prouder," cried his dad with joy. "This is going to be your time to shine. Wear that number eleven shirt with pride. You deserve it!"

Mo grinned to himself, remembering how he'd used to play as Liverpool on the PlayStation as a kid. Now he was playing in the club for real, fulfilling that childhood dream.

LIVERPOOL FC

Nickname: The Reds
Founded: 1892
Stadium: Anfield Stadium
Current league: Premier League
Crest: there have been several iterations of the crest over the years. Currently, the crest used on the players' kits is the liver bird (in either red or white), holding a piece of seaweed in its beak, standing above the club name's initials 'L.F.C.', on a white or red background. The liver bird is a mythical bird that symbolizes the city of Liverpool. It is often represented as a cormorant.

The main crest used on the club's merchandise shows a red liver bird on a shield with the words 'LIVERPOOL FOOTBALL CLUB' above it. Above the shield, in green, sits the top of the Shankly Gates and the words of the club's anthem, 'YOU'LL NEVER WALK ALONE'. On either side of the shield there is an eternal flame in a sconce, in memory of the victims of the 1989 Hillsborough disaster. Under the shield is a green ribbon with the founding date of the club, 'EST.1892'.

21

LIVERPOOL LIFE

Mo, Magi and their daughter settled into their new life in Liverpool.

Jürgen Klopp kept his promise, and Mo made his Liverpool debut in a game against Watford on the opening day of the 2017/18 Premier League season. And Mo kept his promise, scoring one of the three goals of the match.

This was a great start to the season, and Mo found his pace with the team and continued to score goals.

In October 2017, Mo helped Egypt qualify for the 2018 World Cup, their first since 1990. He was becoming an international legend, too. The Egyptian fans loved him. Mo was awarded the 2017 African Footballer of the Year award. At the award ceremony, Mo told the audience that winning it was a childhood dream.

"This is a very special moment for me," Mo said. "I would like to dedicate this award to all the kids in Egypt and Africa, and I want to tell them to never stop dreaming, never stop believing."

Back in Liverpool, the fans were beginning to single out Mo as one of their favourite players. This lad from Egypt played football like a god. Mo's incredible speed and his powerful goal-scoring kicks were becoming the stuff of legends, and the fans loved their new star player.

Liverpool had qualified for the Champions League. Mo seized the moment. He was going to play like his life depended on it and show his team and the fans how thankful he was to be there.

"We're in the semi-final of the Champions League," Mo shouted down the phone to his brother, Nasr. "Can you believe it?"

"The whole village is going to be watching you, Mo," Nasr laughed. "Don't let us down, we're counting on you!"

Liverpool would be playing Mo's old club AS Roma at Anfield. It would be a challenge playing against his old teammates, but Liverpool was his club now and he was going to give it his all for them.

With two goal assists and two fantastic goals, Mo helped put Liverpool in the Champions League final. As Mo left the pitch, the Liverpool fans stood up to clap his world-class performance.

Overwhelmed with joy and pride, Mo turned to the fans and clapped right back. Then, in a rousing chorus, the fans started singing at the top of their voices,

"Mo Salah, Mo Salah, Mo Salah,
Running down the wing.
Salah la la la la la la
The Egyptian king!"

Then they sang another song:
"We've got Salah, do do do do do do!
Mané Mané, do do do do do do,
And Bobby Firmino,
But we sold Coutinho!"

Mo would never forget that moment.

Sadly, Liverpool didn't beat Real Madrid in the final. Mo left the pitch in tears, but he knew he could come back stronger. His fans deserved his best and he was going to give it to them.

22

BECOMING A CHAMPION

Despite a shoulder injury and Egypt being knocked out of the 2018 World Cup in the group stage, Mo continued to impress his fans and team during his second season at Liverpool.

Mo marked his hundredth appearance for Liverpool with two of the five winning goals against Huddersfield Town. The race was on for the Premier League title. Liverpool and their rivals Manchester City were neck and neck all season. But, in the end, Manchester City won – by just one point! Mo was gutted – he had been so close to winning his first Premier League title.

"It should have been ours," Mo told his mum and dad.

"Yes, it should have been," said his mum. "But, son, you're the league's top scorer. Those twenty-two Premier League goals mean a lot. And don't forget your Golden Boot award! Mo, you are the superstar you wanted to be."

"And there's still the Champions League to play for," added Nasr.

As the day of the Champions League final loomed, Mo couldn't contain his excitement.

"This could be it, the moment I have been working towards all my life!"

Liverpool were facing rivals Tottenham Hotspur. It would be a tense game.

When Liverpool were awarded a penalty in the first minute of the game, Mo stepped up to take it. Nothing was going to distract him. With the precision he was famous for, Mo took the kick and BAM! The ball hit the back of the net at speed. The atmosphere in the stadium was electric. Liverpool led 1-0. When Divock Origi made a second goal late on in the game, Liverpool knew they had won.

They were champions of Europe! And Mo's moment had arrived.

"You did it!" he whispered to himself.

23

A STRANGE SEASON

Being a star required dedication and hard work. Mo never forgot this. He knew how quickly someone could fall if they became too complacent, and he was not going to let that happen.

So as his third season at Liverpool kicked off, Mo worked harder than ever. He owed it to himself and that fourteen-year-old boy he had been when he got his first big break playing for Al Mokawloon. Mo had star quality, but he was humble, too. Jürgen Klopp and his Liverpool teammates admired him for that.

"I will never forget where I come from," he

told Mohamed Elneny. "That struggle has made me who I am today. And now I am playing for the best club in the world."

"Well, apart from Arsenal!" laughed Mohamed.

And what a hero Mo was. As 2019 drew to a close, Liverpool won the Club World Cup for the first time in their history, and Mo was voted Best Player of the Tournament. He was racking up the awards!

What a perfect end to the year.

Liverpool were playing well at the start of 2020 and by March they were twenty-five points clear at the top of the league table. Then the unthinkable happened.

Covid-19 struck, and the world shut down.

Like everyone else, Mo was concerned about his family and friends, and Magi was pregnant with their second child. Nagrig seemed like a million miles away now that he couldn't travel home. Football was suspended and life as everyone knew it stopped.

In June, the UK government said football matches could be played again. But one important factor was missing. The fans couldn't go to the games. It still wasn't safe for big crowds of people to mix, and they could only watch their heroes play on TV.

For the footballers themselves it was very odd. There was no atmosphere in the stadiums and the games felt flat.

"It's horrible playing without our fans to cheer us on," sighed Mo when he chatted on the phone to Mohamed.

"I know," replied Mohamed. "But we have to be safe."

When Chelsea beat Manchester City in their game in late June, Liverpool became the Premier League champions. Because they were so many points ahead, there was no way any of the other teams could catch them up. They had won the Premier League with a record-breaking seven games in hand. What a strange victory. This was Liverpool's first league title for thirty years.

Mo had never imagined he would win his first Premier League title to empty stadiums and no cheering fans.

24

FOOTBALL LEGENDS

EGYPTIAN KING

The beautiful game returned once again, and the fans were back at the games.

Mo clocked up another impressive season during 2021/22, with thirty-one goals over fifty-one appearances. His contract was coming up for renewal, and the football world was buzzing with speculation. Would this superstar stay with Liverpool? But Mo had no intention of leaving the club that was helping him achieve his life-long dreams.

"I've signed a new three-year deal," Mo told his dad excitedly. "I want to keep playing for Liverpool."

Mo was now Liverpool's highest paid player in the club's history. He was world famous and people talked about his brilliant performances on the pitch and his charitable deeds outside of football.

Being in the very fortunate position of having lots of money, Mo wanted to give some of it back to help ordinary people, not only in his little village but all over Egypt and in other African countries. He had been given so many opportunities with the support of his family, and he wanted other kids to be able to dream like him and achieve those dreams.

The kids in Mo's home village idolized him. They flocked to the local café to watch Liverpool games and stuck posters of him everywhere.

"You're our Egyptian king!"

As the 2022/23 season rolled around, Mo broke the thirty-goal barrier for his third season running. He was making a name for himself as one of football's 'Big Three'. Along with Roberto Firmino and Sadio Mané, these three greats were the most lethal attacking trio on the pitch.

By the summer of 2023, many clubs around the world wanted to sign Mo. The Saudi team

Al Ittihad bid an astonishing one-hundred-and-fifty million to take Mo, but Liverpool declined. They were not going to sell their star who was the Premier League's top scorer again, with eighteen goals.

At the start of 2024, Mo picked up a hamstring injury in the African Cup of Nations tournament, which ended his involvement.

"I'm sorry I'm not going to be able to play with you this time," Mo told Mohamed Elneny.

"Yeah, Mo, how are we going to manage without you?" sighed Mohamed. "You're our star player."

Mo was disappointed. He loved playing for his country. But he had to return to Liverpool to begin his rehabilitation. The injury was worse than the club had first feared. Mo couldn't play for a month, and then after one game, he suffered another setback and was out for a further three weeks.

Mo was frustrated. "I didn't think it would take me so long to get my form back," he complained to his family. The season wasn't going well for him.

"Give yourself time, son," his dad said. "You'll find your goal-scoring feet again.

While Mo worked on his fitness and

rehabilitation, some unexpected news came.

Jürgen Klopp announced that he was leaving Liverpool. He would step down as manager at the end of the 2023/2024 season. The team were in shock. Mo couldn't believe it. What was going to happen to them? Klopp's retirement could change everything.

And Mo's contract was coming up for renewal again. Would he stay this time if someone was prepared to pay the right price?

But when Arne Slot was announced as the club's new manager, Mo was happy to stay, and Arne was more than happy to keep him.

As the 2024/2025 season kicked off, Mo felt his confidence returning. His fitness was back and he was determined to do well for the club, his new manager and his fans. However difficult things got, Mo was never one to give up, the mark of a true superstar.

"You've got so much more to offer," Arne told Mo. "Liverpool needs you; the fans need you."

Mo smiled his famous smile. "I love this club and the fans, and I want to keep playing for as long as I can. I'm not going anywhere."

With a second Premier League title win to his name, Mo was looking forward to the 2025/26 season.

Liverpool's Egyptian king was here to stay.

Mo Salah's Timeline

15 June 1992	Mohamed Salah Hamed Mahrous Ghaly is born in Nagrig, a small farming village in Egypt.
2004	Mo's dad takes him for a trial with Ittihad Basyoun football club. Mo joins the club. This is the start of his youth football career. A scout from Al Mokawloon spots Mo and invites him to play in another youth team in Tanta.
2006	Mo joins the youth team at Al Mokawloon.

May 2010	Mo signs a contract with Al Mokawloon to join their senior squad. This is the start of his career in professional football, playing in the Egyptian Premier League.
25 December 2010	Mo scores his first senior goal against Al Ahly in the Egyptian Premier League. The final score is 1-1.
September 2011	Mo has his international debut, playing for Egypt in the Under-20 World Cup in Colombia.
October 2011	Mo scores his first senior international goal for the Under-23 Egypt team in the Africa Cup of Nations qualifiers against Niger. Egypt secure a place in the 2012 Olympic Games in London.
June 2012	Basel football club signs Mo for two-and-a-quarter million pounds.
July/August 2012:	Mo scores three goals, one in each of Egypt's group games at the Olympic Games.

January 2013	Basel football club signs Mohamed Elneny, Mo's best friend.
11 April 2013	Mo scores his first Europa League goal as Basel beat Tottenham Hotspur in the quarter-final second leg.
18 September 2013	Mo scores the first goal to equalize with Chelsea in the Champions League group stage. Basel go on to win this match.
26 November 2013	Basel beat Chelsea again in the Champions League group stage, with Mo scoring the winning goal.
17 December 2013	Mo marries his childhood sweetheart, Magi Sadeq.
January 2014	Chelsea football club sign Mo for eleven million pounds. Mo moves to England. He doesn't get to play in many matches, and he loses his confidence.
2014	Mo and Magi's first daughter, Makka, is born.

February 2015	Chelsea loan Mo to Fiorentina football club. He moves to Italy, where he starts scoring goals again and regains his confidence and passion for the game.
2015	Chelsea loan Mo to AS Roma at the end of the season. He has a fantastic season with them.
25 October 2015	Mo is sent off the pitch for the first time in his professional football game in a match against his former team Fiorentina.
3 August 2016	AS Roma sign Mo for thirteen-and-a-half million pounds.
6 November 2016	Mo scores his first ever career hat-trick at club level in a match against Bologna. The final score is AS Roma 3-0 Bologna.
July 2017	Liverpool sign Mo for 43.9 million pounds – their most expensive signing at the time.
12 August 2017	In Mo's debut match for Liverpool against Watford he scores his first goal for his new team.

October 2017	Mo helps take Egypt to the World Cup in their qualifier game against Congo. This is the first time Egypt have played in the World Cup since 1990.
24 October 2018	Mo scores his fiftieth goal for Liverpool in the Champions League group stage against Red Star Belgrade. Liverpool win the game 4-0.
8 December 2018	Mo scores his second hat-trick for Liverpool football club.
26 April 2019	In Liverpool's Premier League game against Huddersfield, Mo makes his hundredth appearance for Liverpool.
1 June 2019	Liverpool win their sixth Champions League title 2-0 against Tottenham Hotspur. Mo scores one of the two winning goals when he takes a penalty.

21 December 2019	Liverpool win the Club World Cup 1-0 in the final against Flamengo. This is the first time in their history that Liverpool have won this cup. Mo is voted Best Player of the Tournament.
2019/20 season	Mo is Liverpool's top goal scorer in this season.
2020	Mo and Magi's second daughter, Kayan, is born.
March 2020	Liverpool are twenty-five points clear at the top of the league, then Covid-19 strikes, and there is no football until June 2020. Fans are not allowed to attend any of the matches.
25 June 2020	Liverpool win their first Premier League title with a record-breaking seven games to play. This is their first league title in thirty years.
2022	Mo signs a new three-year deal with Liverpool football club. He becomes the highest-paid player in the club's history.

2022/23 season	Mo breaks the thirty-goal barrier for the third season running. In an away game to Rangers in the Champions League, Mo scores a hat-trick in seven minutes!
2024	Saudi team Al Ittihad bid one-hundred-and-fifty million pounds to take Mo, but Liverpool decline.
26 January 2024	Jürgen Klopp announces his decision to step down as Liverpool's manager at the end of the season.
1 June 2024	Arne Slot becomes the new Liverpool manager.
2024/25 season	Mo is Liverpool's top goal scorer.
January 2025	Mo has to drop out of the African Cup of Nations tournament due to a hamstring injury.
25 April 2025	Liverpool win their second Premier League title.

Mo's Clubs

2006-2012: Al Mokawloon Al Arab Sporting Club

Nicknames: Arab Contractors (after the company that founded the club)
Founded: 1973
Stadium: Osman Ahmed Osman Stadium, also known as the Arab Contractors Stadium

2012-2014: FC Basel 1893

Nickname: FCB, RotBlau (RedBlue, their home colours)
Founded: 1893
Stadium: St Jakob-Park

2014-2016: Chelsea FC

Nickname: The Blues
Founded: 1905
Stadium: Stamford Bridge

2015: ACF Fiorentina (on loan from Chelsea)

Nicknames: La Viola (the Purples), I Gigliati (the Lilies)
Founded: 1926
Stadium: Artemio Franchi Stadium

2015-2016 (on loan from Chelsea), transfer 2016-2017: AS Roma

Nicknames: I Giallorossi (the Yellow and Reds), I Lupi (the Wolves), La Magica (the Magic One)
Founded: 1927
Stadium: Stadio Olimpico

Summer 2017–present : Liverpool FC

Nicknames: The Reds
Founded: 1892
Stadium: Anfield Stadium

National team 2011–present : Egypt

Nicknames: the Pharaohs, Mother of the World team, Africa's Giants
Founded: 1921
Stadium: Cairo International Stadium

Team Honours

Swiss Super League (with FC Basel): 2012/13, 2013/14

UEFA Champions League (with Liverpool): 2018/19

UEFA European Super Cup (with Liverpool): 2019

FIFA Club World Cup (with Liverpool): 2019

Premier League (with Liverpool): 2019/2020, 2024/2025

FA Cup (with Liverpool): 2022

English Super Cup (Community Shield) (with Liverpool): 2022

English League Cup (with Liverpool): 2022, 2024

Individual Honours

Players' Player of the Year Award: 2017/2018

African Footballer of the Year Award: 2017, 2018

BBC African Footballer of the Year: 2017, 2018
FWA Footballer of the Year: 2018, 2022, 2025

PFA Player of the Year: 2018, 2022

Premier League Golden Boot: 2018, 2019, 2022, 2025

In 2019 Time Magazine named Mo as one of the world's most influential people.

Premier League Playmaker of the Season: 2022

Premier League Record Breaker

Mo had an outstanding first season playing for Liverpool in the Premier League in 2017/18:

- He made thirty-six appearances for Liverpool.
- He scored thirty-two goals, the most ever scored in a thirty-eight-game season at the time.
- He was the first African player to score thirty goals in a Premier League season.
- He was the first player to score in twenty-four separate Premier League games.
- In addition to his goals, Mo helped with eleven assists.
- He was the first player to win the Player of the Month Award three times in a season.
- He was voted Premier League Player of the Year.
- He was voted Players' Player of the Year.
- He was voted Football Writers' Association Player of the Year.
- He won the Golden Boot in his first season.

Club Record Breaker

- In his debut season at Liverpool (2017/18), Mo scored forty-four goals in all competitions – a Liverpool record for a debut season.

- Between 2017 and 2019 he scored the most goals – sixty-nine – after one hundred Liverpool appearances.

- He was voted Best Player of the Tournament in the Club World Cup which Liverpool won.

Sensational Salah Facts

Nickname: the Egyptian king, the Pharaoh

Height: 1.75 metres

Position: Forward/right winger

Mo is **left-footed**.

There are pictures of Mo all over his home village of **Nagrig, Egypt**, and a mural of him in **Times Square, New York City, USA.**

Mo has several well-known pitch goal celebrations – including the **yoga man**, the **Egyptian king** and **the prayer**.

In his spare time, Mo does **yoga, plays video games** and enjoys **table tennis**.

He's been called the **Egyptian Messi**.

Mo never forgets where he came from. He donates **millions** of pounds to charities in Egypt and around the world.

At AS Roma, Mo had been more of a winger than a striker; with his amazing sprint speed, he could race past defenders and set up chances. Jürgen Klopp helped turn Mo into a forward and a **goal-scoring machine**.

Dubbed **'the Big Three'**, Mo Salah, along with Roberto Firmino and Sadio Mané, were one of the world's most **lethal** attacking trios.

Mo Quotes

Mo Salah is known for his inspirational quotes, which reflect his positive outlook on life, his gratitude for all his blessings, his strong work ethic and his perseverance and ambition. What he says reveals his passion for and dedication to football.

"When I get a chance to go back to my village, I always remind myself where I came from."

"I want to be the best player in the history of Egyptian football."

“I give all my life to football; I only think about football. This is what is on my mind all the time.”

“We’re just human beings. In the end, you do your job. I do my job in the best way I can.”
“I always try to see my weakness, work on it, to be better as a person and a player, everything.”

“Every year, every day, every month I am proving myself.”

“I miss many chances, but I always keep trying, and sometimes you score easy goals or difficult goals, but in the end, I am trying to score.”

On winning the Premier League title in 2025:
“It is incredible to win this with our fans. This is one hundred per cent better than last time, especially with the fans. We have a different group now so to show we can do it again is something special.”

Also available in the Football Legends series:

FOOTBALL LEGENDS
KYLIAN MBAPPÉ
Ed Hawkins
FOOTBALL LEGENDS
LIONEL MESSI
E. L. Norry

FOOTBALL LEGENDS
COLE PALMER
Ben Lerwill

FOOTBALL LEGENDS
ERLING HAALAND
Ben Lerwill

FOOTBALL
LEGENDS
JUDE BELLINGHAM
Paul Stewart

OTBALL
EGENDS
BUKAYO SAKA
Ben
Lerwill

FOOTBALL LEGENDS
VINÍCIUS JÚNIOR
George Maudsley

CRISTIANO RONALDO
George Maudsley

FOOTBALL LEGENDS
GARETH SOUTHGATE
E. L. Norry
RAHEEM STERLING
Musa Okwonga